Moving From Brokenness to Victory

"Overcoming the World through Poems"

Georgia Loraine Clarke

Moving From Brokenness to Victory Copyright © May 2016 by Georgia Loraine Clarke Published in the United States of America by

www.gospel4unetwork.com

All rights reserved. No part of this book may be reproduced or transmitted in anyway by means, electronic, mechanical, Photocopy, recording or otherwise, without prior permission of the author except as provided by USA copyright law.

Scriptures are taken from the King James Version unless otherwise marked.

ISBN - 9780692697047
Library of Congress Control Number 2016906850

Printed in United States of America
May 2016

GEORGIA LORAINE CLARKE

Content

FOREWORD
INTRODUCTION

Part 1 – Where Do I Go?.................................13
    Where Do I Go?
    Your Word My Light
    Before Me
    When?
    I Don't Understand

Part 2 – In Times of Trouble.........................31
    Time of Trouble
    Treacherous Friend
    Discombobulated
    Paternal Absence
    So Much Rain
    In the Fire
    I Am a Nobody – to God be the Glory
    Introvert
    God Seems Silent

Part 3 – Coping with Pain...........................67
    Escape
    Today
    Give Me Faith
    Like Eagles

Soaring Above the Storm
Sometimes
If the Foundations Be Destroyed
Lost Focus of Him
Help Comes from God
Don't Hate Your Haters
My Name is Wisdom
Live in the Moment
As I See It
When I Place All My Trust in God
Persevere
Be Positive
Little Fixes
Life Goes On
Live One Day at a Time
Stability and Change

Part 4 – Hope...137
Hope
The Heavenly Visitor
Yes, Jesus Loves Me
Everything on Earth is Only Temporary

Part 5 – Salvation 149
A Seed is Planted
Follow Me
Obey and Believe
Before Any Resting
It's Not Easy to Warn
Like the Snake
Salt of the Earth
Light to Heaven
Possess Me with Your Spirit

Because God Loves He Gave
Call Things That Are Not as Though They Were
Rewarder
Beautiful Again

Part 6 – At Peace...193
    Happy in this Place
    Thank God
    Assuming My Purpose
    My Happy Place

References

MOVING FROM BROKENNESS TO VICTORY

Foreword

Poetry is a divine language! God loves poetry. No wonder why more than one-third of the Bible is written in poetry. This includes entire books (except for short prose sections), such as Job, Psalms, Proverbs, the Song of Solomon, and Lamentations. The first words man ever uttered were poetry (cf. Genesis 2:23).

Through poems, we express our thoughts, feelings, and actions in artistic ways that surpass prose or narrative. This is why I recommend *From Brokenness to Victory* as inspirational collection of poems that will take you through life's diverse experiences with a focus on the love of God in Christ. This book portrays the ups and downs of life that we face on a daily basis, and expresses victory over life's troubles by looking at the beauty of God's redemptive work for us.

My advice to you is: do not read this book all at once! It is too much to take in one sitting. The richness of life experience in these poems requires pausing and reflection on our part. Read one poem at a time and think through it before you move on to the next one. Meditate on the Scriptures at the top of every poem as you ponder the words of the poem itself.

I pray that as you read this book you can see your own journey and relate to the author's experience with the goal of tasting God's sweet love in overcoming our difficult circumstances.

Gospel 4 U Network Team

GEORGIA LORAINE CLARKE

Introduction

This book is a collection of poems that helped me through some hard periods in my life as I learn on a daily basis how to deal with painful issues. One particular poem in this book, "*A Seed is Planted*," was written when I was faced with things that I thought were too impossible for me to handle in this world. Although it's about planting a seed and waiting for the harvest, when I wrote it, I was actually thinking about my life. I believe that everything in life initiates from a seed, but before reaping, the seed must first be planted. However, the seed takes time to grow, but in order for a seed to grow, it first has to change. A seed doesn't stay a seed forever. It changes during the germination process. This process requires some damp soil, high temperature, sunlight, water, and most importantly, it must have an outside source to nourish and care for it. So, yes, a seed undergoes change. Then it takes a new form. Whether it will manifest into a flower or a fruit, each seed changes into something new in order for it to become a supplement to life. A seed just doesn't get to that point of maturity overnight. It takes time. It takes transformation.

Subsequently to the transformation, its beauty will be unfolded for the world to behold and enjoy.

During long periods of trials in my life, I began to acknowledge that growing is a process. The change that I needed in my temporal life was to let go of my horrific past and embrace the change that was about to come. I had to believe that I would eventually take a better form after the process ends, even if it takes time. Time though can go on forever, but harvest will ultimately come.

So often we spend long periods of time waiting for change to come, not realizing that we have to face the reality of going through the process. We want to experience changes, but we don't want to go through the waiting process. When things didn't go the way I planned, I would spend so much time being impatient, frustrated, angry, and disappointed. Finally, I realized that things only happen in God's timing and I can't argue the fact that God's timing is always perfect, can I?! So we have to accept God's timing. Just as a seed is hidden in the ground, and we believe that it's maturing somehow, it's the same way with our lives. Sometimes we just have to wait for the harvest and while we wait we have to continue to believe that the change is coming. We can't lose hope. We must have faith!

Yes, it takes faith to make it through the waiting process. We have to believe that there is something more to life than the norm. There is supernatural force that rules the universe—that surpasses all man's understanding—this is the outside source that is there to nurture to a point of maturity. When things seems impossible in life, we have to remember that God can do anything He wants on this earth, but He only does it in His own time. God made a way through the sea for His people. He provided water in the desert for them. This we must remember when we come upon a dry season in our lives—God can run water in the dessert places of our lives. We just have to believe and wait. Don't give up. A change must come!

MOVING FROM BROKENNESS TO VICTORY

Part 1

Where Do I Go

MOVING FROM BROKENNESS TO VICTORY

"For I know the thoughts that I think toward you, saith the LORD, thoughts of peace, and not of evil, to give you an expected end. ^{12} Then shall ye call upon me, and ye shall go and pray unto me, and I will hearken unto you. ^{13} And ye shall seek me, and find me, when ye shall search for me with all your heart."
(Jeremiah 29:11–13)

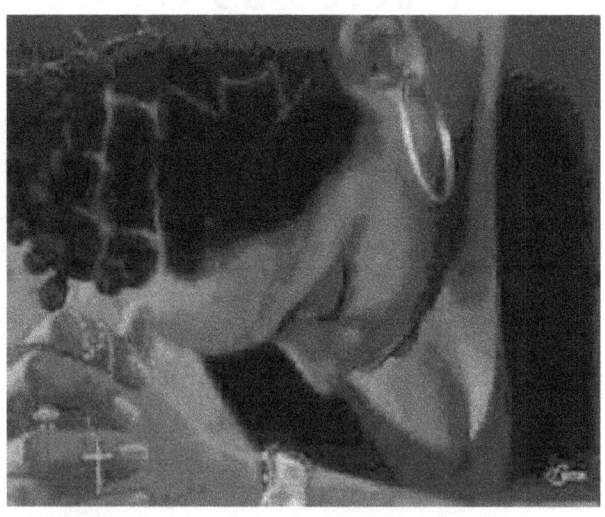

Where Do I Go?

Where do I go when things look dread,
When dreams seem dead,
When help is far away,
When there's night for day?

If I go to the Maker who's bigger than my pain,
He will stop the rain,
Turn night into day,
Roll burdens away.

No one can tell me that I can't receive,
If I only believe,
In the unseen,
Call things into being.

"Thy word is a lamp unto my feet, and a light unto my path."
(Psalm 119:105)

Your Word My Light

Sometimes I wonder how I'll make it through,
Because things just seem so impossible.
As I scan through the tedious road ahead,
I wish for a cot on which to lay my head,
And a bailout for all the debts I owe.
Speculating when I'll have that afterglow,
The light that remains after the sun has set,
When will all my basic needs be met?

So I whispered a prayer to the Lord above,
And He whispered back to me with love.
He said, "Don't think of the path that you will go,
The right path in time to you I'll show.
Don't wonder what it is you're going to do,
Just see the One who'll take you through.
Let My Word be your guiding light,
No matter how dark the gruesome night."

I said, "Lord Your Word I clearly hear,
But will You please minimize my fear?
Give me wisdom to take me where
I'm eased from all my pain and care.
That I can overcome my fright,
To walk by faith and not by sight.

That Your Word may be my guiding light,
No matter how dark the gruesome night."

GEORGIA LORAINE CLARKE

"And the LORD went before them by day in a pillar of a cloud, to lead them the way; and by night in a pillar of fire, to give them light; to go by day and night: He took not away the pillar of the cloud by day, nor the pillar of fire by night, from before the people."
(Exodus 13:21–22)

Before Me

I have to get up and start my day,
But before I do I have to pray.
I need God before me to guide my way,
Cause if I go alone, I'll surely stray.

There's darkness before me, I need His light.
Unending battles, I'll need Him to fight.
I need His presence in the midst of my fright,
Because when He's around everything is alright.

Crooked paths before me, only He can make straight,
Crush iron bars before me that are blocking the gate.
Show me the right road that will lead to my fate,
And keep me secure in a "granite state."

So before I get up to start my day,
The one thing I have to do is pray.
I will need God before me to guide my way,
If I do it alone, I will surely stray.

GEORGIA LORAINE CLARKE

"Humble yourselves therefore under the mighty hand of God, that he may exalt you in due time: Casting all your care upon him; for he careth for you. Be sober, be vigilant; because your adversary the devil, as a roaring lion, walketh about, seeking whom he may devour."
(1 Peter 5:6–8)

GEORGIA LORAINE CLARKE

When?

So many miles behind,
Miles already travelled.
Gone in space and time,
With people and events.
They're unpleasant places,
Unfamiliar places,
Dark places, haunted places.
Where does it end?
Oh, I long to reach,
That place in my dreams,
Where satisfaction finds me.
Pressing forward but it seems,
Road blocks are countless,
Detours are endless.
The road of rejections,
Is forever in sight.
The way to deception,
Is as dark as the night.
There's no iridescent light,
No warm inviting nights,
Under starry skies.
When will I reach,
That place of pure delight?
That deepens me,
My very being caress.
When will I find,

That place of happiness?
I feel a familiar presence,
Holding me up,
Shielding me from harm.
In a cold place, yet warm,
It'll be ok then, I guess.
He knows everything best.
Still I ask when?
When will I see,
That place called Glee?
I ask when?
When will I reach,
That place of peace?
When will I hear,
That liberty bell?
There's only one answer:
Time will tell.

GEORGIA LORAINE CLARKE

"So then faith cometh by hearing, and hearing by the word of God."
(Romans 10:17)

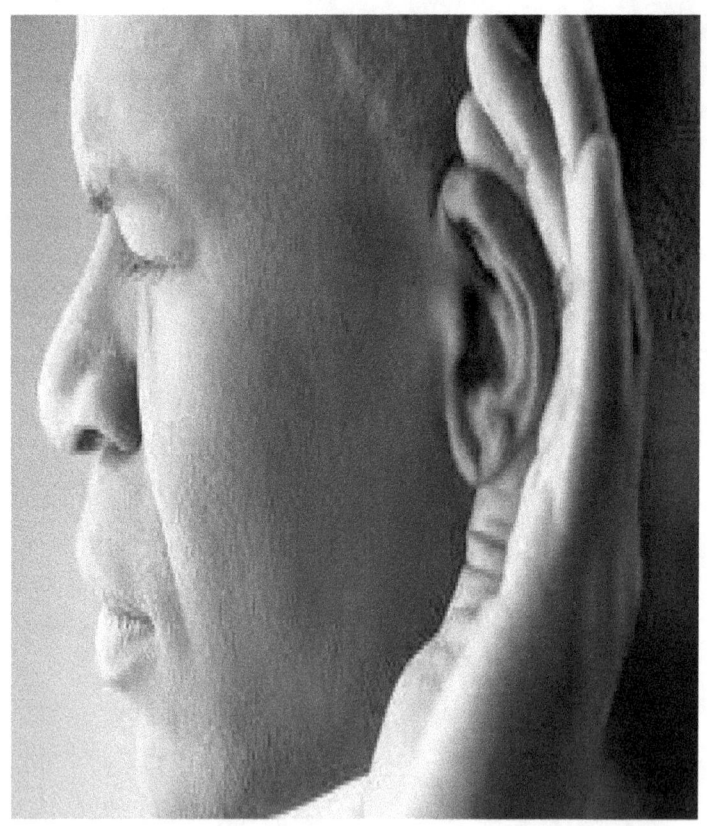

I Don't Understand

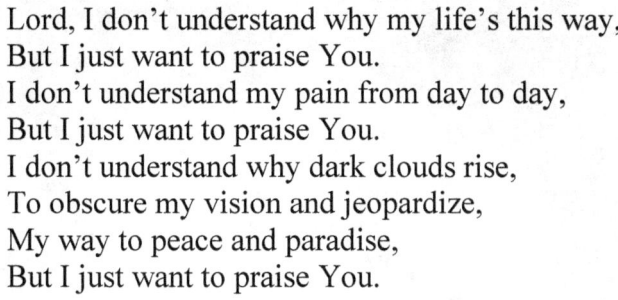

Lord, I don't understand why my life's this way,
But I just want to praise You.
I don't understand my pain from day to day,
But I just want to praise You.
I don't understand why dark clouds rise,
To obscure my vision and jeopardize,
My way to peace and paradise,
But I just want to praise You.

Lord I don't understand why things look so impossible,
But I just want to praise You.
I don't understand the persistent obstacles,
But I just want to praise You.
Although sometimes I feel afraid,
To caper into life's escapades,
And meet annoying barricades,
Still I want to praise You.

Lord, I don't understand this thing called "faith,"
But I just want to praise You.
I don't understand how to bear this heavy weight,
But I just want to praise You.
I'll pursue till You Words are clear to me,
Circumstances seem hopeless, but I will see.
I'm just one "hearing" away from my victory,
So I want to praise You.

Part 2

Times of Trouble

"Although the fig tree shall not blossom, neither shall fruit be in the vines; the labour of the olive shall fail, and the fields shall yield no meat; the flock shall be cut off from the fold, and there shall be no herd in the stalls: Yet I will rejoice in the LORD, I will joy in the God of my salvation. The LORD God is my strength, and he will make my feet like hinds' feet, and he will make me to walk upon mine high places."
(Habakkuk 3:17–19)

Time of Trouble

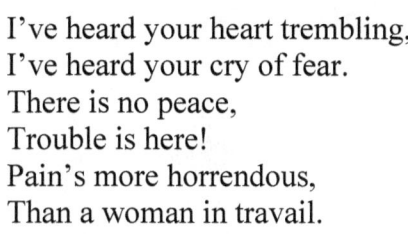

I've heard your heart trembling,
I've heard your cry of fear.
There is no peace,
Trouble is here!
Pain's more horrendous,
Than a woman in travail.
Your heart is wounded,
Your face is turned pale.

But do not fear,
Don't be dismayed.
For I am with you,
And you shall be saved.

Your bruises are incurable,
Your wounds are great.
There is none to heal,
You're losing faith.
Your sorrow's irrepressible,
No help is near.
You are totally forgotten,
Your case is severe.

But do not fear,
Don't be dismayed.
For I am with you,
And you shall be saved.

For all your afflictions,
Why do you cry?
There is none to save,
Nor on whom to rely.
They call you an outcast,
A spoil and a prey.
But I will have mercy,
In the latter days.

So do not fear,
Don't be dismayed.
For I am with you,
And you shall be saved.

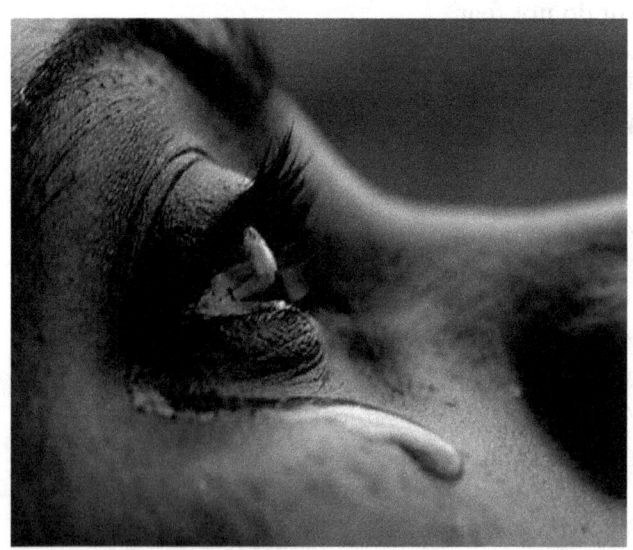

GEORGIA LORAINE CLARKE

"He that hateth dissembleth with his lips, and layeth up deceit within him; When he speaketh fair, believe him not: for there are seven abominations in his heart. Whose hatred is covered by deceit, his wickedness shall be shewed before the whole congregation."
(Proverbs 26:24–26)

Treacherous Friend

Lord, please do not forget about me,
Please do not ignore my plea.
I'm disturbed by the things they say about me,
With resentment the enemy attacks me,
Inflicting excruciating pain upon me,
Making malicious threats towards me.
My heart mourns out in deep agony,
Horrors of darkness has come over me.

Oh if I could flea!
Oh if I could flea!
Make an escape to a place,
Where no one recognizes me.
Far away from the tempest,
Far away from the stress,
Make an escape to a place,
To a place of sweet rest.

Can't stay in this city,
Where prowls violence and strife.
Can't stay in this city,
Where wickedness secretly hides.
They're setting snares on the sly,
Mischief-makers bring misery,
Destructive forces bring lies,

Pretenders' deceit and haters bring guile.

Oh that they may seize!
Oh that they may seize!
But unceasingly, obstinately,
They parade the streets.

If it were an enemy who betrayed me,
That I could tolerate.
If it were an enemy who rose against me,
I could have hidden away.
But it was you, the one I would always defend,
The one who walked with me daily pretending to be my friend.
It was you, we even worshiped together among the flock,
and when you have any problem,
For you my very back I would bend.

My confidant deceives his friend,
Violating the trust, the bond is tainted.
With lyrics that were much sweeter than honey,
But heart filled with jealousy and hatred.
For years and years you had up-stored,
You had charms that could not be bought with money.
Yet in my back you had a drawn sword.

If it were an enemy who betrayed me,
That I could tolerate.
If it were an enemy who rose against me,
I could have hidden away.

But it was you, the one I would always defend,
The one who walked with me daily pretending to be my friend.
It was you, the one I cared for greatly,
It was you, my close friend.

You know God does not sleep,
His eyes are never closed,
He sees every deed.
Every evil He'll oppose,
Every action He'll reward,
Every fate He'll diagnose.
He will take you by surprise,
One day there'll be no repose.
He will recompense your lies,
All your evil He'll expose.
And right in your face,
Heaven's gates He will close.

"These things I have spoken unto you, that in me ye might have peace. In the world ye shall have tribulation: but be of good cheer; I have overcome the world."
(John 16:33)

Discombobulated

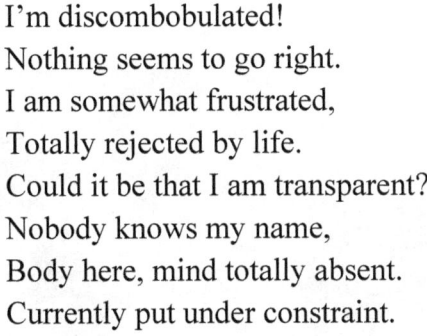

I'm discombobulated!
Nothing seems to go right.
I am somewhat frustrated,
Totally rejected by life.
Could it be that I am transparent?
Nobody knows my name,
Body here, mind totally absent.
Currently put under constraint.

Every day is another battle,
Another dreaded hill to climb.
Life seems like a constant struggle,
No joy, no peace of mind.
Intentional racial injustice,
Is white superior to black?
The inward hurt goes unnoticed,
Oh, if my mind one could hack!

Pain would be recognizable,
Tears like a river would flow.
The scars and the culprits describable,

But silence permits no one to know.
Silence can't be misquoted,
Silence construed as "the fool."
But silence is completely devoted,
Cause silence allows God to rule.

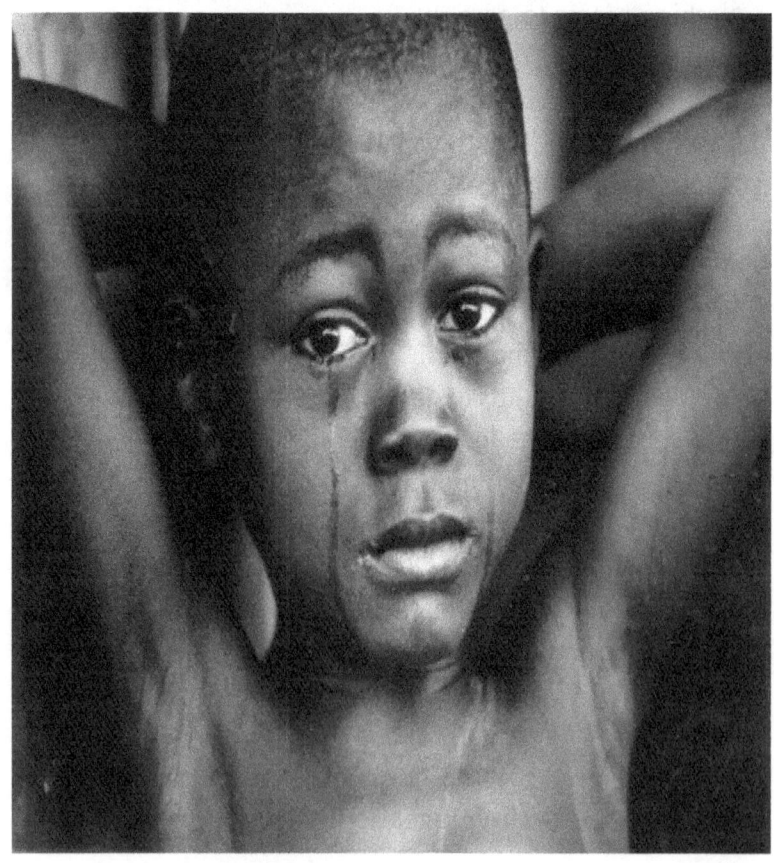

GEORGIA LORAINE CLARKE

"...thou hast been my help; leave me not, neither forsake me, O God of my salvation. When my father and my mother forsake me, then the LORD will take me up."
(Psalm 27:9–10)

Paternal Absence

Years of silence,
Since he was five.
Father missing,
Don't know if he's dead or alive.
Years of torture,
Not knowing what's true.
Needed his father,
Didn't know what to do.

Silent torture,
Misunderstood.
Maternal disaster,
Affections a few.
Stepfather drama,
One after the next.
None better than the other,
Pure emptiness.

Internal torture,
Can't show what's real.
Internal anger,
Don't know what to feel.
Paternal absence,
A boy needs a man,
A paternal presence,
Rock on which to stand.

MOVING FROM BROKENNESS TO VICTORY

Years of torture,
Not knowing what's true.
A boy needs his father,
To guide him on through.
Years of silence,
Since he was five.
Paternal absence,
Don't know if he's dead or alive.

GEORGIA LORAINE CLARKE

"And God shall wipe away all tears from their eyes; and there shall be no more death, neither sorrow, nor crying, neither shall there be any more pain: for the former things are passed away."
(Revelation 21:4)

GEORGIA LORAINE CLARKE

So Much Rain

My life is filled with so much pain,
I see less sunshine so much rain.
Makes my body feel so drained,
Heartstrings absolutely strained.

There's so much rain!
There's so much rain!
Please, let the sun come out again!

I'm not supposed to ask God why,
I'm not supposed to sit and cry.
So how can I this hurt deny?
My dreams just always pass me by.

There's so much rain!
There's so much rain!
Please, let the sun come out again!

Lord, forgive me if I am wrong.
I am so weak, Lord, make me strong.
If I to You, dear Lord, belong,
Please, keep me if my pains prolong.

There's so much rain!
There's so much rain!
Please, let the sun come out again!

MOVING FROM BROKENNESS TO VICTORY

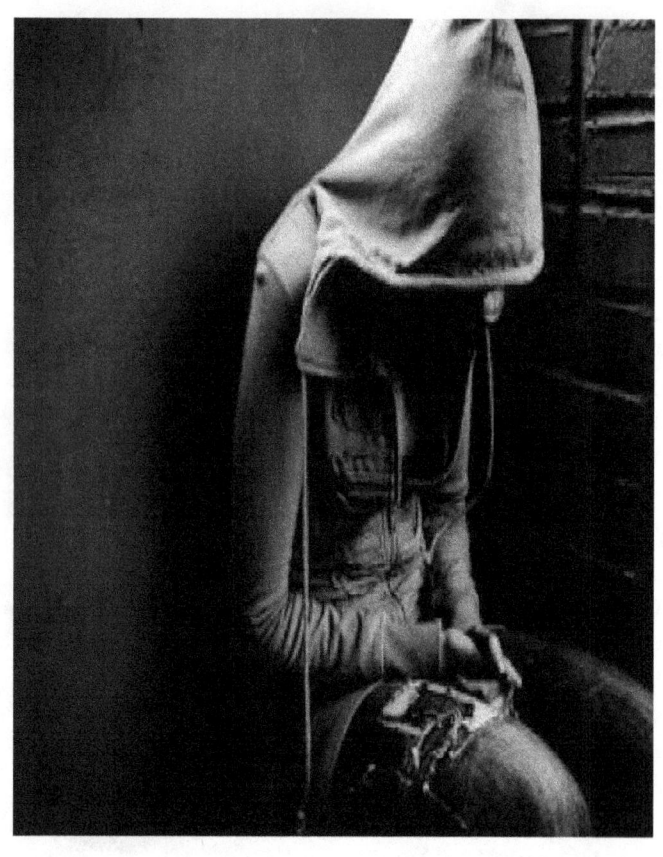

GEORGIA LORAINE CLARKE

"Then was Nebuchadnezzar full of fury, and the form of his visage was changed against Shadrach, Meshach, and Abednego: therefore he spake, and commanded that they should heat the furnace one seven times more than it was wont to be heated. And he commanded the most mighty men that were in his army to bind Shadrach, Meshach, and Abednego, and to cast them into the burning fiery furnace. Then these men were bound in their coats, their hosen, and their hats, and their other garments, and were cast into the midst of the burning fiery furnace. Therefore because the king's commandment was urgent, and the furnace exceeding hot, the flame of the fire slew those men that took up Shadrach, Meshach, and Abednego. And these three men, Shadrach, Meshach, and Abednego, fell down bound into the midst of the burning fiery furnace. Then Nebuchadnezzar the king was astonied, and rose up in haste, and spake, and said unto his counsellors, Did not we cast three men bound into the midst of the fire? They answered and said unto the king, True, O king
(Daniel 3:19–24)

In the Fire

One more time I'm in the fire,
But I shall not be burned.
Thrown in the fire by the enemy,
Fire darts at every turn.
Thrown in the fire cause of jealousy,
But I shall not be burned.
I shall not be burned, you see,
For God's with me in the fire.

> They threw me in the blazing fire,
> The furnace by the minute is higher.
> But I shall not be burned, you see,
> For God's with me in the fire.

The ones who threw me in this fire
They shall be destroyed.
The flame is blazing on the wire,
This snare for me deployed.
The furnace by the minute is higher,
But I shall not be burned.
I shall not be burned, you see,
For God's with me in the fire.

> They threw me in the blazing fire,
> The furnace by the minute is higher.
> But I shall not be burned, you see,

For God's with me in the fire.

They shall be scorched by their very own snare,
Against me they conspire.
Its set for me they were unaware,
The rage of the ravenous fire.
They did me in without a cause,
My ruins they desire.
But I shall not be burned, you see,
For God's with me in the fire.

> They threw me in the blazing fire,
> The furnace by the minute is higher.
> But I shall not be burned, you see,
> For God's with me in the fire.

"But unto them which are called, both Jews and Greeks, Christ the power of God, and the wisdom of God. Because the foolishness of God is wiser than men; and the weakness of God is stronger than men. For ye see your calling, brethren, how that not many wise men after the flesh, not many mighty, not many noble, are called: But God hath chosen the foolish things of the world to confound the wise; and God hath chosen the weak things of the world to confound the things which are mighty; And base things of the world, and things which are despised, hath God chosen, yea, and things which are not, to bring to nought things that are: That no flesh should glory in his presence."
(1 Corinthians 1:24–29)

I Am a Nobody – to God be the Glory

I am a nobody,
I am so unworthy,
Of Jesus' sweet mercy and grace.
I'm nothing without Him,
So hopeless without Him,
My sins with His beauty replaced.

Not many mighty,
Not many noble,
Are called for the service of Christ.
God called the harlot,
God called the Gentile,
The base things which are despised.

God chooses the humble,
God chooses the lowly,
For God alone must be idolized.
Came not for the righteous,
But sinners to repentance,
For His mission to be utilized.

Where is the wise?
Where is the scribe?
No flesh will glory in His presence.
God chooses the weak,
God chooses the meek,

The meek to be filled with His essence.

God uses the dumb,
God uses the blind,
Foolish things to confound the wise.
I am a nobody,
To God be the glory,
He sees the base things which are despised.

GEORGIA LORAINE CLARKE

"And he said unto me, My grace is sufficient for thee: for my strength is made perfect in weakness. Most gladly therefore will I rather glory in my infirmities, that the power of Christ may rest upon me."

(2 Corinthians 12:9)

Introvert

I am an introvert, I must confess,
For this reason, I have faced many tests.
Civilization believes that my quietness
Should be interconnected with mere weakness.
And likewise they see my inaudibility
As a perfect example of stupidity.
There're also those who see me as a mystery,
Because they can't actually see through me.
Do I have to come up with some kind of strategy
To reveal that I'm more appealing than they care to see?

I do admire the extroverts who can speak up a storm,
On any topic, in any group or in any form.
While I'd need a bit more time to articulate my opinions,
Before I can come out with a distinct expression.
And I'm not as outgoing as the regular folks,
I am reserved, soft spoken, and that's no joke.
So they think I am lacking in some capacity,
Or maybe I possess some kind of deficiency.
They think I'm slow and deprived of velocity,
I'm not vivacious or filled with vitality.

But should I be underestimated for who I am?

Should I be judged, discredited, or looked down upon?
Should I reveal that there's more to me than meets the eye?
But what would I have gained from this, even if I try?
I'll be wrestling with this issue till the day I die.
In their eyes, I'm just a stuck-up just because I'm shy.
But frankly, of nothing important I have ever been deprived.
I still live and breathe like everyone else in this life.
And although I've been classed as a misfit in society,
This really has no basis on authenticity.

Still there's an identifying factor of this introvert,
I do less chitchatting, what I do most is observe.
So I know what they think that I do not know,
And I see everything but I don't care to show.
I realize my capabilities and I know my own worth,
Of what it truly means to be an introvert.
I smile to myself as I started believing,
I'm an exquisitely defective human being.
I don't need to hang with the popular crowd,
I'm not ashamed of that, matter of fact I am proud.
I have contentedly accepted this reality,
I am an introvert and that's who I will always be.

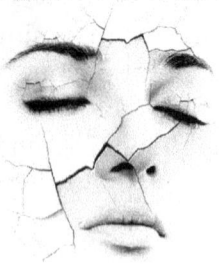

GEORGIA LORAINE CLARKE

> *"Unto thee will I cry, O LORD my rock; be not silent to me: lest, if thou be silent to me, I become like them that go down into the pit....*
> *Blessed be the LORD, because he hath heard the voice of my supplications. The LORD is my strength and my shield; my heart trusted in him, and I am helped: therefore my heart greatly rejoiceth; and with my song will I praise him."*
> **(Psalm 28:1, 6–7)**

God Seems Silent

God seems silent.
A silence that I can feel,
A silence that makes me wonder,
God, are You for real?

God seems silent.
A silence that lasts longer than a moment,
I'm patiently holding still,
Totally yielded to His will.

God seems silent,
A silence that last longer than a day.
Does God hear me when I pray?
Does He have anything to say?

God seems silent.
A silence that last longer than a year,
Um… God are you still there?
Come on, I know that You care!

God seems silent.
A silence that lasts longer than forever.
Lord, please look down from Thy throne,
Please don't leave me here all alone!

Time is of the essence,
Am I still in His presence?

Did He cancel His agreements?
Did He manifest such an intent?

Then…

Finally, He speaks.
He speaks through my mind.
My purpose is divine,
Perfect and sublime.
It's just a matter of time,
Only a matter of time.

Part 3

Coping With Pain

"There hath no temptation taken you but such as is common to man: but God is faithful, who will not suffer you to be tempted above that ye are able; but will with the temptation also make a way to escape, that ye may be able to bear it."
(1 Corinthians 10:13)

"Get thee behind me, Satan."—*Luke* iv. 8.

Escape

It is not good
For a man to be alone.
Then why do my scars convert
My heart into a stone?

Isolating myself,
I live in a bubble.
Isolating myself,
From all of life's trouble.

Looking for an escape,
To a place of less torture.
Where there's no memories of the past,
No thoughts of the future.

I discovered a place,
That's bitterer than death.
There're snares and chains,
Seductions and nets.

Neurotransmitter acting
Slow in the brain.
Serotonin sluggish,
Energy drained.

There's a supernatural world,
Where things are not seen.

MOVING FROM BROKENNESS TO VICTORY

Yet the things that are not,
Can be called into being.

I discovered a place,
Where burdens are laid.
Faith was applied,
The moment I prayed.

There is an escape,
To a place of no torture.
No memories of the past,
No thoughts of the future.

Here in this place,
I humbly relent.
In whatever state I am,
There with to be content.

GEORGIA LORAINE CLARKE

"Rejoice evermore. Pray without ceasing. In every thing give thanks: for this is the will of God in Christ Jesus concerning you."
(1 Thessalonians 5:16–18)

Today

Lord, help me today
To be positive in everything,
No matter how hopeless they seem,
No matter how dark the valley's been,
No matter how high the mountains grow,
No matter how hard the winds may blow.

Lord, help me today
To give thanks in everything.
For the good as well as the bad,
For when I am happy or when I am sad.
When I get discouraged, Lord, help me to note,
That life is a mixture of both.

Lord, give me faith today
To trust you always in everything,
During the times when I'm walking tall,
Or the times when my back is against the wall.
And, Lord, when I find myself in whatever state,
Never to waiver in my faith.

"For this is the love of God, that we keep his commandments: and his commandments are not grievous. For whatsoever is born of God overcometh the world: and this is the victory that overcometh the world, even our faith. Who is he that overcometh the world, but he that believeth that Jesus is the Son of God? This is he that came by water and blood, even Jesus Christ; not by water only, but by water and blood. And it is the Spirit that beareth witness, because the Spirit is truth."

(1 John 5:3–6)

Give Me Faith

Lord, please take away my fears,
Give me faith.
Lord, please to keep me in your care,
Give me faith.
Lord, when I'm blinded by my tears,
Help me to see You standing there.
That I Your voice will clearly hear,
Give me faith.

I want to overcome the world,
By believing in Your Word.
So Your light won't be obscured,
Give me faith.

Lord, when I'm saddened by my pain,
Give me faith.
Lord, let my heart sing once again,
Give me faith.
When my sunshine turns to rain,
And my life becomes a strain,
Let Your joy in me remain,
Give me faith.

I want to overcome the world,
By believing in Your Word.
So Your light won't be obscured,
Give me faith.

MOVING FROM BROKENNESS TO VICTORY

Let me be pleasing in Your sight,
Give me faith.
What's wrong in me, Lord, make it right,
Give me faith.
In the middle of my fight,
Turn my darkness into light.
When I'm frozen by my fright,
Give me faith.

I want to overcome the world,
By believing in Your Word.
So Your light won't be obscured,
Give me faith.

GEORGIA LORAINE CLARKE

"But they that wait upon the LORD shall renew their strength; they shall mount up with wings as eagles; they shall run, and not be weary; and they shall walk, and not faint."
(Isaiah 40:31)

Like Eagles

I believe that everything will work itself out,
No matter what tempest life brings.
Endless wait makes it easy to be coerced into doubt,
But I'll keep my gaze on the unseen things,
All of the promises of God,
Until they manifest for everyone to see.

God whispered to me while I relentlessly prayed.
He said, "Strength is gained while you wait,
Use the storm like the eagle to keep you stayed.
No matter what fury the storm dictates,
Morning brings sunrise for warmth,
And time that'll eventually strengthen and renovate."

I refuse to be diminished by the storms of life.
Directed by the creator on high.
Although the wind, the lightning, and the rain do rife,
Sleek with torrents, and roaring of the thunder nearby,
I'll find a high point to wait.
Then dive in head on to mount up with wings like eagles.

"Doth the eagle mount up at thy command, and make her nest on high? She dwelleth and abideth on the rock, upon the crag of the rock, and the strong place. From thence she seeketh the prey, and her eyes behold afar off. Her young ones also suck up blood: and where the slain are, there is she."
(Job 39:27–30)

Soaring Above the Storm

An eagle knows when a storm is approaching,
Long before it breaks.
The eagle would fly
Up high on a summit,
And wait for the storm to break.

The eagle then positions its wings to be lifted
High above the storm.
Below the storm rages,
Above the eagle is drifted,
Soaring on top of the storm.

Instead of avoiding the storm, the eagle uses the storm
To be graceful, stable and sure.
The eagle uses the storm
To be lifted higher,
Rising on the winds of the storm.

Like an eagle we can face the storms of our lives.
Being patient, stable and sure,
When the winds lift us up.
Our strength is revived,
Then above the storm we can soar

MOVING FROM BROKENNESS TO VICTORY

GEORGIA LORAINE CLARKE

"When thou passest through the waters, I will be with thee; and through the rivers, they shall not overflow thee: when thou walkest through the fire, thou shalt not be burned; neither shall the flame kindle upon thee. For I am the LORD thy God, the Holy One of Israel, thy Saviour: I gave Egypt for thy ransom, Ethiopia and Seba for thee."
(Isaiah 43:2–3)

Sometimes

Sometimes I'm thrown in the lion's den,
My foes like loins want to rip me to threads.
"I will keep you," Lord, that's what You said.
So instead of fearing the lions. I see You instead,
When I'm thrown in the lion's den.

Sometimes I'm thrown in the furnace of fire,
Furnace seven times hotter than it's supposed to be,
To make sure that I burn beyond degree.
But I insist that my God will deliver me,
When I'm thrown in the furnace of fire.

Sometimes I'm thrown in the middle of the battle.
Challenger's equipped with giant so tall,
Heave insults and ridicules because I'm so small.
Being small with a big God I can conquer all,
When I'm thrown in the middle of the battle.

Sometimes I'm stranded in the eye of the storm,
I see Jesus come walking on top of the sea,
He extended His hand and He said, "Come to me."
If only I could focus on Him with whom I want to be,
I won't sink when I'm stranded in the storm.

MOVING FROM BROKENNESS TO VICTORY

GEORGIA LORAINE CLARKE

> *"But without faith it is impossible to please him: for he that cometh to God must believe that he is, and that he is a rewarder of them that diligently seek him."*
> **(Hebrews 11:6)**

If the Foundation Be Destroyed

You tell me to be realistic,
That my dreams can't be fulfilled.
You ask me why I am so idealistic,
When I leave all to God, now I'm still.
You ask me why I take so many chances
In a world of vagueness and gloom.
Do you really think that fear I should harness,
When God assured me He would come soon?

Faith is that foundation.
Yet faith you falsely construe.
Faith is what my salvation is built on,
So then why make faith seem untrue?
And if I should destroy that foundation,
Then what can the righteous do?

You say, "Run to the mountains for safety,"
When God is my one protection,
When the foes aim their arrows to shoot me.
You say, "Get away from their Gatling gun."
I believe that God watches me closely,
And every battle He's won.
He said He would never leave me lonely,
So why would you tell me to run?

MOVING FROM BROKENNESS TO VICTORY

Faith is that foundation.
Yet faith you falsely construe.
Faith is what my salvation is built on,
So then why make faith seem untrue?
And if I should destroy that foundation,
Then what can the righteous do?

"Now it came to pass, as they went, that he entered into a certain village: and a certain woman named Martha received him into her house. And she had a sister called Mary, which also sat at Jesus' feet, and heard his word. But Martha was cumbered about much serving, and came to him, and said, Lord, dost thou not care that my sister hath left me to serve alone? bid her therefore that she help me. And Jesus answered and said unto her, Martha, Martha, thou art careful and troubled about many things: ^{42} But one thing is needful: and Mary hath chosen that good part, which shall not be taken away from her."
(Luke 10:38–42)

Lost Focus of Him

Are you anxious and troubled over many things,
And sometimes frustrated by the worries life brings?
You're not even aware
That Jesus is presently
Standing right there,
Because you've lost focus of Him?

Do you feel like Jesus is unaware of your cares?
Are you disheartened by all the burdens you bear?
So you worry and fret,
And Jesus you often
So easily forget,
Because you've lost focus of Him.

Do you feel like you have to do life all by yourself,
You feel all alone like there's no one to help,
You do not recall,
God's vow to be there,
In whatever befall,
Because you've lost focus of Him?

Do you take on errands God didn't ask you to do,
Then complain that these tasks are just too much for you,
No wisdom to know,
Of pointless little habits.

You need to let go,
Because you have lost focus of Him?

Are you dictating to God how your life should unfold?
If God would see things your way and do what He's told,
Thinking you can command
God into granting
Your selfish demands,
Because you have lost focus of Him?

Lord, I realize that I have lost sight of Thee.
Let me refocus my attention on what's necessary.
Forgive me, I pray.
And help me to follow,
In Your footsteps today,
That I will never lose focus of Thee.

GEORGIA LORAINE CLARKE

"I will lift up mine eyes unto the hills, from whence cometh my help. My help cometh from the LORD, which made heaven and earth. He will not suffer thy foot to be moved: he that keepeth thee will not slumber. Behold, he that keepeth Israel shall neither slumber nor sleep. The LORD is thy keeper: the LORD is thy shade upon thy right hand. The sun shall not smite thee by day, nor the moon by night. The LORD shall preserve thee from all evil: he shall preserve thy soul. The LORD shall preserve thy going out and thy coming in from this time forth, and even for evermore."
(Psalm 121)

GEORGIA LORAINE CLARKE

Help Comes from God

Many a times
I find myself
In the wilderness
I need some help!

I look behind,
I see my foes,
Approaching fast
Where do I go?

In front of me
There's the big Red Sea.
On either side
There's mountains spree.

I have no choice
But to look up.
Look to the hills
To fill my cup.

Help comes from God,
From God above.
That's where I find
My one true love.

He makes a pathway

MOVING FROM BROKENNESS TO VICTORY

Through the sea.
Water through desert,
He runs for me.

My foes pursue
Still after me.
He drowned them all,
In the big Red Sea.

So now I know,
I know that He,
O, yes, I know,
That He loves me.

GEORGIA LORAINE CLARKE

"And no marvel; for Satan himself is transformed into an angel of light."
(2 Corinthians 11:14)

Don't Hate Your Haters

What if you find out that your biggest ally
Was really that person on whom you shouldn't rely?
Because that person just talks you up in front of you,
But has no reservations putting a dagger in your back too.

What do you do when he would scandalize your name,
And consistently, calculatingly would bring you to shame?
What if the one who seems like he's lifting you up
Was actually the one pulling you down and won't stop?

First, you must identify whom you're really dealing with.
It's not the hater, but the devil who wants to get you to quit.
The devil hides behind the hater, deception's his favorite tool.
So don't get angry at your hater, let the Word of God rule.

MOVING FROM BROKENNESS TO VICTORY

Fighting with your haters is not really your job
God will do the fighting so your joy won't be robbed.
Pay no attention to you haters, stick to your mission
Can't afford to lose sight of your destination.

You fight against God when you fight against me
Remember Pharaoh drowned in the great Red Sea
Remember Goliath the giant how he lost his head.
Herod also tried, but worms got him instead.

GEORGIA LORAINE CLARKE

"Forsake her not, and she shall preserve thee: love her, and she shall keep thee. Wisdom is the principal thing; therefore get wisdom: and with all thy getting get understanding."
(Proverbs 4:6–7)

My Name is Wisdom

Hello, my name is wisdom.
I dwell with prudence.
I seek out knowledge and witty inventions.
I, wisdom, fear the Lord.
Therefore, I hate evil,
As well as pride and arrogance.
Wayward mouth I also hate,
But with knowledge and understanding I can relate.

When God prepared the heavens,
I, wisdom, was there.
When there was no depth, I was brought forth.
When He appointed the foundations,
Rejoicing in the habitable portions,
Going east, west, north, and south,
I, wisdom, was His daily delight.
I travelled with Him both day and night.

Knowledge is attainable through experience.
But I, wisdom, act appropriately upon it.
When knowledge sees trouble brew,
I, wisdom, completely avoid it.
Knowledge memorizes the Word of truth,
I, wisdom, actually obey it.
So ask God to bless greatly with wisdom,
For with knowledge there must be caution.

MOVING FROM BROKENNESS TO VICTORY

GEORGIA LORAINE CLARKE

"Take therefore no thought for the morrow: for the morrow shall take thought for the things of itself. Sufficient unto the day is the evil thereof." **(Matthew 6:34)**

GEORGIA LORAINE CLARKE

Live in the Moment

From seconds to minutes,
From minutes to hours,
And the hours divide up the day.
Once the day is past,
It can't be undone.
So live each moment the best possible way.

Time can't be re-winded,
Fast-forward or paused.
Memories can't be deleted or destroyed.
Create memories of love,
Compacted with peace,
Animosity and jealousy avoid.

Don't grieve over the past,
Because the past is gone,
And will never break the surface again.
Don't fear the future,
Because it is not yet come.
Let God do it so you won't go insane!

From seconds to minutes,
From minutes to hours,
And the hours divide up the day.
Once the day is past,
It can't be undone.
So live each moment the best possible way.

MOVING FROM BROKENNESS TO VICTORY

GEORGIA LORAINE CLARKE

"Hast thou entered into the treasures of the snow? or hast thou seen the treasures of the hail, Which I have reserved against the time of trouble, against the day of battle and war? By what way is the light parted, which scattereth the east wind upon the earth? Who hath divided a watercourse for the overflowing of waters, or a way for the lightning of thunder; To cause it to rain on the earth, where no man is; on the wilderness, wherein there is no man; To satisfy the desolate and waste ground; and to cause the bud of the tender herb to spring forth? Hath the rain a father? or who hath begotten the drops of dew? Out of whose womb came the ice? and the hoary frost of heaven, who hath gendered it? The waters are hid as with a stone, and the face of the deep is frozen."
(Job 38:22–30)

GEORGIA LORAINE CLARKE

As I See It

As I see it, life comes with different kinds of weather.
Sometimes there's sadness and sometimes some pleasure.
Sometimes you awake to a bright sunny day,
Makes you feel like your troubles are all gone away.
The birds are chirping, the grass is green,
The temperature perfect, the air is clean.
And no matter how much you wish these days would stay,
These glorious days don't ever last always.

Sometimes life comes with those daunting days,
When the storms just continue to rage and rage.
The lightning a flashing, the thunder a rolling,
So outrageously loud, makes you feel so afraid.
You look through the window you see the rain a pouring,
And all of your plans have to be delayed.
You wish for the sun to show up again,
But it seems like the storms will never end.

Then there are the days of blizzards of snow.
Low-hanging clouds as the gusty winds blow.
Power outages leave you alone in the dark,
Through the shadowy path you wish for a spark.
Sometimes you're snowed in and can't get out,

Sometimes through the storm you're up and about.
Finds you stuck in a place so rigidly cold,
Car spinning its wheel at the side of the road.
You wait and you wait for assistance to come,
But it seems like you're indefinitely stuck in the dump.

So as I see it, life comes with all kinds of weather.
And now and again you get a little pleasure.
And what a day brings you will never know,
But whatever that is God allows it so.
Life's unpredictable and there's no doubt,
Sometimes you have to sit and wait things out.
Leave it all to God cause at the end of the day,
When it comes to the weather God has the last say!

GEORGIA LORAINE CLARKE

"The LORD is my rock, and my fortress, and my deliverer; my God, my strength, in whom I will trust; my buckler, and the horn of my salvation, and my high tower."
(Psalm 18:2)

GEORGIA LORAINE CLARKE

When I Place All My Trust in God

Everything that happens in my life,
No matter how awful it may seem,
And every trial that I've had to face
Provide an opportunity for God to display
His mercy and love in such a way
That surpasses all man's understandings.

That's why I make it my duty to trust in God,
Though sometimes many things don't go my way.
And even when traces of darkness appear,
I try not to lean on doubts and fear.
For I know there's a blessing for me somewhere,
And God gets the glory in the end.

So I free myself of this heavy load,
Taking them daily to God in prayer,
Thanking Him for working in my behalf,
For being my personal shield and staff.
For on Him alone my cares I cast,
And rest in His supernatural peace.

I find when I place all my trust in God,
Not being anxious for anything,
I tap right into an unstoppable force,
That no one and nothing can oppose.
My trials will all make sense in due course,
When I place all my trust in God.

GEORGIA LORAINE CLARKE

"*Blessed is the man that endureth temptation: for when he is tried, he shall receive the crown of life, which the Lord hath promised to them that love him.*"
(James 1:12)

Persevere

Sometimes the one who perseveres
Is the one who deems persistent,
Who through the ups or daunting downs
Remains entirely consistent.
The one who struggles through the tears
To take that next step through the fears,
Who keeps on smiling through the cares
Is the one who truly perseveres.

Sometimes the one who perseveres
Is the one who is committed.
Though storms disrupt the road ahead
To God the way's submitted.
Does not let burdens interfere
And through the pain would bring a cheer.
When others cheat remains sincere
Is the one who truly perseveres.

It's true sometimes we lose the fight,
But one fight shouldn't define us.
Just take that loss as a lesson learned,
We shouldn't let it deprive us.
Each mistake, though will shed a light,
Reveals solutions and brings insights,
And in the end it'll be alright,
Although sometimes we lose the fight.

"Finally, brethren, whatsoever things are true, whatsoever things are honest, whatsoever things are just, whatsoever things are pure, whatsoever things are lovely, whatsoever things are of good report; if there be any virtue, and if there be any praise, think on these things."
(Philippians 4:8)

Be Positive

There may not be an actual reason
To be positive today.
But do you really need a reason
When you can but pray?

The best time to be positive
Is when everything elopes.
Joy doesn't mean no problems,
It's the ability to cope.

You control your every action.
So focus on your strengths.
Take charge of your reactions,
Dealing with people and events

Stay focused on your blessings,
Instead of dwelling on the worst.
Your reward will absolutely come,
If you just put God first.

So don't go looking for a reason
To be positive today.
Even in hostile situations,
Be positive anyway.

MOVING FROM BROKENNESS TO VICTORY

GEORGIA LORAINE CLARKE

MOVING FROM BROKENNESS TO VICTORY

"Keep thy heart with all diligence; for out of it are the issues of life."
(Proverbs 4:23)

Little Fixes

When everything is shattered in your life,
When nothing seems to be going right,
When foes insist to bring on strife,
And your home seems like a toxic waste site,

Ok, so this is what you shouldn't do.
Don't tackle the mountains all at once,
Don't let frustrations dominate you,
Don't procrastinate or stay in a trance.

Take each moment as an opportunity
To make a small investment in yourself.
Little fixes each day will incredibly
Take your sense of pride back off the shelf.

It's these little fixes that will take you far
On that road to restitution and recovery,
Make you shine like the diamond that you are
To that place of a new discovery.

"Brethren, I count not myself to have apprehended: but this one thing I do, forgetting those things which are behind, and reaching forth unto those things which are before, I press toward the mark for the prize of the high calling of God in Christ Jesus."
(Philippians 3:13–14)

Life Goes On

Mistakes happen.
Everybody makes them.
The faster they're identified,
The faster they can be rectified.
Mistakes often can be so agonizing,
But turn to experiences after realizing.
Conviction is the core element to success.
When you take initiative to clean up the mess,
Find methods on how to take the good with the bad,
To smile when you're sad, and be glad for what you had,
Soaring above insignificant matters to make clearer your visions,
Recognizing that preventing old mistakes is vital for better decisions.
People do hurt, but forgive them and also yourself and don't you ever forget

MOVING FROM BROKENNESS TO VICTORY

To learn from your mistakes, becoming shrewder
into living a life without regrets.
Don't fail to implement all that you've learned
using each mistake as a conversant lesson,
For days bring changes, roads have sharp turns, but
stay focused and remember that life goes on.

GEORGIA LORAINE CLARKE

MOVING FROM BROKENNESS TO VICTORY

"This is the day which the LORD hath made; we will rejoice and be glad in it."
(Psalm 118:24)

GEORGIA LORAINE CLARKE

Live One Day at a Time

Don't worry about tomorrow,
Let tomorrow take care of itself.
Each day has enough troubles of its own,
Why bring more burden on yourself?

You can't be anxious over yesterday,
Because yesterday is gone.
So why waste moments of your time,
Stressing what's already done?

Consequently, the one true way to live
Is to live one day at a time.
In each day just tackle the work God gives,
With all your energy, heart, and mind.

Don't waste one portion of your day
To leave any work undone.
Accept God's will, don't back away,
Complete with the setting sun.

Then you can rest when the night is come,
The next day in God's hands.
With assurance say, "God my work is done,
I've adhered to Your commands

"Therefore whosoever heareth these sayings of mine, and doeth them, I will liken him unto a wise man, which built his house upon a rock: And the rain descended, and the floods came, and the winds blew, and beat upon that house; and it fell not: for it was founded upon a rock. And every one that heareth these sayings of mine, and doeth them not, shall be likened unto a foolish man, which built his house upon the sand: And the rain descended, and the floods came, and the winds blew, and beat upon that house; and it fell: and great was the fall of it."
(Matthew 7:24–27)

GEORGIA LORAINE CLARKE

Stability and Change

I have learned from life that stability and change,
Where they're concerned, there's no fixed range.
As life goes on they would fluctuate
To make things worse or renovate,
Whichever way life says.

Sometimes when life is going great,
The daunting shift comes and dislocates,
Hauling me out of my comfort zone.
Frustrations now seem overgrown,
Faced with the great unknown.

But I realize change is just momentary.
Everything in life is just temporary.
I've learned to make better choices with each day.
And by faith pass fears along the way,
More aware of what to face.

The choices I make affect my entire life.
So I walk in peace and avoid every strife.
I'll utilize change to enrich my stride.
Until stability comes, I'm taking the ride
To wherever God may lead.

I can't speed up God's plan or slow it down.

MOVING FROM BROKENNESS TO VICTORY

I can't even turn the clock around.
The effects of change may not be stress-free,
But it repaired, strengthened, and characterized me,
Into who I became today.

Part 4

Hope

"By whom also we have access by faith into this grace wherein we stand, and rejoice in hope of the glory of God. And not only so, but we glory in tribulations also: knowing that tribulation worketh patience; And patience, experience; and experience, hope: And hope maketh not ashamed; because the love of God is shed abroad in our hearts by the Holy Ghost which is given unto us."
(Romans 5:2–5)

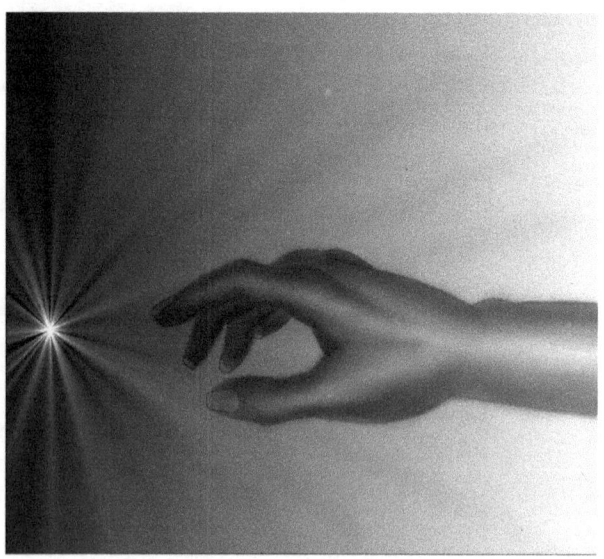

GEORGIA LORAINE CLARKE

Hope

Sitting here alone in the dark,
The only light is just a spark,
Frustrations want to override my faith,
For every opportunity, it seems I'm late,
Completely paralyzed by fear,
Partially blinded by my tears,
Overwhelmed by means of endless rejections,
Can never seem to reach my destination,
In a state of hopelessness,
A place of gloom and loneliness.

I would have fainted, but I believed
The goodness of God my heart received.
In the dark, I see His face,
I'm not alone in this rigid race!
The Lord, my Shepherd, in the night.
He's my salvation and my light.
The Lord, my righteousness and peace,
Only He can cause the storm to cease.
Troubles endure but for a night,
But joy will come with the morning light.

"He putteth my feet in the stocks, he marketh all my paths. Behold, in this thou art not just: I will answer thee, that God is greater than man. Why dost thou strive against him? for he giveth not account of any of his matters. For God speaketh once, yea twice, yet man perceiveth it not. In a dream, in a vision of the night, when deep sleep falleth upon men, in slumberings upon the bed; Then he openeth the ears of men, and sealeth their instruction, That he may withdraw man from his purpose, and hide pride from man."
(Job 33:11–17)

The Heavenly Visitor

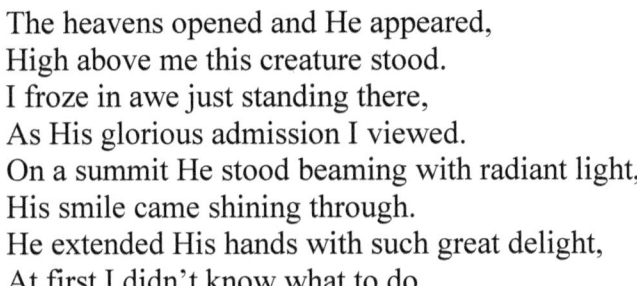

The heavens opened and He appeared,
High above me this creature stood.
I froze in awe just standing there,
As His glorious admission I viewed.
On a summit He stood beaming with radiant light,
His smile came shining through.
He extended His hands with such great delight,
At first I didn't know what to do.

He prepared a golden staircase from Him to me,
With just the sway of His hands.
I ran from the bottom to the top with glee,
My heart with joy did expand.
As I reached to the top I leaped into His arms,
Freed from all my troubles and cares.
In its cradles He rocked me, so safe and warm,
Oh what a time we both shared.

I saw two ladies approaching from the church I attend,
I attempted to greet them, thought I should.
He said, "Child, be careful, they are enemies not friends,
They go to church, but they're evil not good."
With His body He covered me just like a tent
To protect from my friend-enemies.
I couldn't believe He from heaven, was sent

To shield me and watch over me.

He took my hand gently and we sauntered along,
Through valleys, over mountains and plains.
With joys overflowing my heart sang a song,
Relieved from all worries and strains.
I found myself walking in front for a while,
Then suddenly He pulled me back.
He said, "Sinking sand's ahead like a pathway beguiled,
Awaiting to subtly attack."

Oh I was blind, I was blind to it all.
But my Savior, He so knew the way.
He saw all the dangers that await to befall,
Directing me, saving the day,
Then He told me to just walk in His footsteps behind,
In each footprint meticulously.
For He already knows all the dangers to find,
And again said, "My child follow me."

Then He showed me a wonderful mansion sublime,
Decked with pearls and rubies and gold.
All the colors so splendid, magnificent, divine,
Oh what delight to behold!
I was humbled that He chose me to show me this place.
I am nothing yet He highly esteemed.
I was awaken – I was angry – I was red in the face,
Realizing it was only a dream.

But unexpectedly I drifted right back into sleep.

Amazed! He there waiting for me.
He said, "You're not alone, I'm all yours to keep,
So where did you go? Why did you leave?"
Overwhelmed by His kindness on His shoulders I cried,
Such affection so sweet and sublime.
He embraced me so gently, my tears He then dried,
In His bosom sweet comfort to find.

He took me to a garden, it's fragrant so sweet,
So softly its stream flowed along.
Oh what a bliss! Peace and joy was complete,
With Him nothing could ever go wrong.
All the night long we both sauntered together,
Oh I wish that this night wouldn't end.
but I knew from that moment I would always remember,
This is the best night that I'll ever spend.

"Greater love hath no man than this that a man lay down his life for his friends."
(John 15:13)

Yes, Jesus Loves Me

Yes, I'm making a strong declaration.
Yes, I affirm that it's true.
Yes, all that may happen in my desperations.
Yes, Jesus I owe all to You.

Jesus, my God and my Creator,
Jesus, who rules everything.
Jesus, who conquered death in His own power,
Jesus' love died for our sins.

Love, it was love who died on that cross.
Love put Himself in my place.
Love was imparted to me just because,
Love, sins for me were erased.

Me, love on me, filthy me, He bestowed.
Me, so unworthy of Love.
Me, love to me, though unworthy, He showed,
Me, sent to me from above.

Me, like a sheep, like a sheep gone astray,
Me, filled with iniquity,
Me, who had turned just to walk my own way,
Me, yes, Jesus loves me!

MOVING FROM BROKENNESS TO VICTORY

"For which cause we faint not; but though our outward man perish, yet the inward man is renewed day by day. For our light affliction, which is but for a moment, worketh for us a far more exceeding and eternal weight of glory; While we look not at the things which are seen, but at the things which are not seen: for the things which are seen are temporal; but the things which are not seen are eternal."
(2 Corinthians 4:16–18)

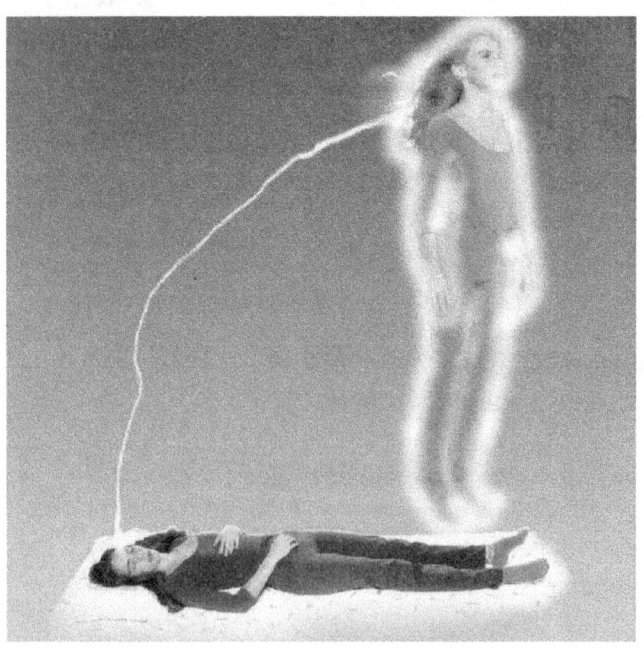

Everything on Earth is Only Temporary

Every time there's a storm,
The storm eventually ceases.
Every time you get hurt,
The hurt eventually heals.
After every night,
There comes a new day.
So the night doesn't never
Ever last always.

So live for the moment,
Enjoy all the fun.
Everything may change,
When the day is done.
But when things are bad,
You don't have to worry.
Cause everything on earth
Is only temporary.

When life isn't easy,
That doesn't mean you can't smile.
Don't let a little hardship
Slowly cramps your style.
Every day comes along,
With a new beginning.
When the day's finally done,

You'll have a new ending.

So live for the moment.
Enjoy all the fun.
Everything may change,
When the day is done.
But when things are bad,
You don't have to worry.
Cause everything on earth
Is only temporary.

Part 5

Salvation

"Let us not be weary in well doing: for in due season we shall reap, if we faint not."
(Galatians 6:9)

A Seed is Planted

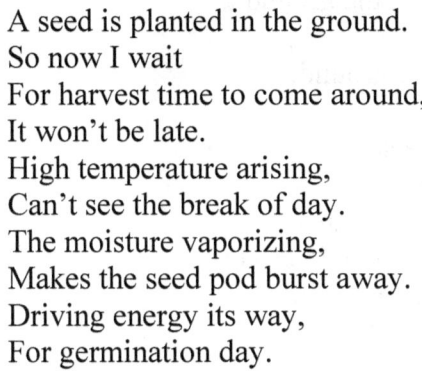

A seed is planted in the ground.
So now I wait
For harvest time to come around,
It won't be late.
High temperature arising,
Can't see the break of day.
The moisture vaporizing,
Makes the seed pod burst away.
Driving energy its way,
For germination day.

The seed is hidden in the ground,
No one can see it.
The roots are slowly shooting down,
That's how time has it.
Roots are pushing through the soil,
Stems bit by bit materializing,
Growing from the seedling coiled.
Now it's photosynthesizing,
And aiming for the sun,
Germination's finally done.

A tiny plant emerges from the ground,
This all took time.
It has finally broken forth unbound,
The wait expired.
Was a slow and steady process,
Yet not late one single day.

I patiently waited for the promise,
These steps don't happen right away.
But in it's perfect time,
Heads for the finish line.

A seed was planted in the ground,
I didn't see it.
It was maturing underground,
I just believed it.
I distinguished that a seed was sown,
Waiting was a heavy load.
It took a while till it was grown,
I thought my patience would erode,
Harvest didn't come that fast,
But then it came at last!

GEORGIA LORAINE CLARKE

"Take heed that ye do not your alms before men, to be seen of them: otherwise ye have no reward of your Father which is in heaven. Therefore when thou doest thine alms, do not sound a trumpet before thee, as the hypocrites do in the synagogues and in the streets, that they may have glory of men. Verily I say unto you, They have their reward. But when thou doest alms, let not thy left hand know what thy right hand doeth: That thine alms may be in secret: and thy Father which seeth in secret himself shall reward thee openly."
(Matthew 6:1–4)

Follow Me

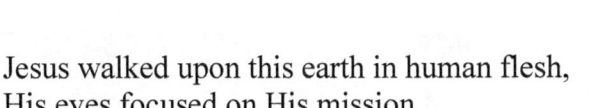

Jesus walked upon this earth in human flesh,
His eyes focused on His mission.
He never came to be seen of men or to impress,
Humbly betrothed to submission.

Jesus never lost sight of His assigned purpose,
He knew what he came to do.
Everywhere He went His good works surplus,
Sacrificing all the way through.

To those whom He chose He told, "Follow Me,"
They surrendered His call to obey.
With tenderness led, with compassion He fed,
His disciples continued that way.

Then was His ultimate sacrifice made,
He died for the sins of the world.
With His own life He gave, our debts were all paid
By Jesus the only Good Shepherd.

So how do we follow in His footsteps today?
He's still pleading, "Come follow me."
Our brother is hungry, we don't give, we don't pray,
Ignoring the brother in need.

MOVING FROM BROKENNESS TO VICTORY

We live in a world that's self-centered today,
Nobody really cares about the other.
What happens to helping someone by the way?
Are we truly the keeper of our brother?

GEORGIA LORAINE CLARKE

"Fear thou not; for I am with thee: be not dismayed; for I am thy God: I will strengthen thee; yea, I will help thee; yea, I will uphold thee with the right hand of my righteousness."
(Isaiah 41:10)

Obey and Believe

Everything in life is attainable,
There's nothing I can't achieve.
If I only put my trust in God,
If I only obey and believe.

All doubts and fears must be erased,
To successfully set my dreams in place.
But in all of this I have to know,
I must allow God to run the show.

God does everything in His own time,
Not a day sooner, not a day behind.
While some don't trust in His existence,
Each day, make sure, I'm in His presence.

God always has a plan in place,
But the major element is faith.
God cannot lie, so I am still,
My desires He promised to fulfill.

So everything in life is attainable,
There's nothing I can't achieve.
If I only put my trust in God,
If I only obey and believe.

MOVING FROM BROKENNESS TO VICTORY

GEORGIA LORAINE CLARKE

"There remaineth therefore a rest to the people of God. For he that is entered into his rest, he also hath ceased from his own works, as God did from his. Let us labor therefore to enter into that rest, lest any man fall after the same example of unbelief."
(Hebrews 4:9–11)

Before Any Resting

Before receiving,
There must be believing.
Before any resting,
There must be some working,
So we have to labor,
To be worthy of rest.
And our faith must be tried,
To prove we can stand the test.

Before believing,
There must be some hearing.
Before overcoming,
There must be some suffering.
So today if you hear,
Don't harden your hearts.
And you can't through temptations,
From your duties depart.

Before any resting,
There must be resisting.
Faith from the beginning,
Must remain to the ending.
Don't be like our forefathers,
Who constantly provoked.
With them God was so grieved,
That their rest He revoked

MOVING FROM BROKENNESS TO VICTORY

> *"But as the days of Noah were, so shall also the coming of the Son of man be. For as in the days that were before the flood they were eating and drinking, marrying and giving in marriage, until the day that Noah entered into the ark, And knew not until the flood came, and took them all away; so shall also the coming of the Son of man be."*
> **(Matthew 24:37–39)**

GEORGIA LORAINE CLARKE

It's Not Easy to Warn

I was talking to a lady just the other day,
She was telling me how evil the world has become.
I said the goodness of mankind would fade away,
Because the coming of the Lord is soon to come.

She said this tale she's been hearing since the day she was born,
Then she laughed in my face and said I was wrong.
With disgust she debated with a look of scorn,
Then mockingly asked, "Is that your theme song?"

She said, "This heaven you mentioned must be such a big place
To fit all of these people who are here on this earth."
I said, "Heaven's prepared for just the ones saved by grace,
Those who chose right over wrong knowing what heaven is worth."

I said, "God is coming back but no one knows the hour,
Like a thief in the night He will surely appear.
In all of His glory, majesty, and power.

He'll judge the earth so we should be prepared."

She walked away saying that she believed not a word,
She said heaven doesn't exist and that Jesus has been dead.
She said all that I'm saying is rather absurd,
If I choose to believe that fable, she said, "You go right ahead."

Then I think to myself that it's not so easy to warn,
The world of this judgement that will come upon the land.
Will I be able to successfully sound the alarm
When no one wants to take heed to the Lord's command?

Now I really recognize how Noah had felt,
One hundred twenty years of preaching seemed all in vain.
Noah must have felt like he was hit below the belt,
Seeing all the people perished when it rained and rained.

GEORGIA LORAINE CLARKE

"And no man hath ascended up to heaven, but he that came down from heaven, even the Son of man which is in heaven. And as Moses lifted up the serpent in the wilderness, even so must the Son of man be lifted up: That whosoever believeth in him should not perish, but have eternal life."
(John 3:13–15)

Like the Snake

Going a long distance around the land of Edom,
Escaping out of Egypt towards the place of freedom,
From Mount Hor they journeyed towards the Red Sea.
They complained and murmured as much as could be,
Out of Egypt you brought us, can you tell us why?
In this loathsome desert, surely we will die.
So God plagued His people with poisonous snakes.
After many perished, Moses prayed for their sakes.
A fiery serpent, God told Moses to make,
Set it on a pole, like a curse on a stake.
A serpent on a pole for your repentance I give,
Everyone who's bitten, when he sees it, shall live.

A man named Nicodemus came to Jesus one night,
Confused about this new birth, he couldn't see the light.
Jesus told Nicodemus, you must be born again.
He couldn't grasp the concept; it was hard to explain.
"As Moses lifted up the serpent in the desert," Jesus said,
"So must the Son be lifted up, to bring life to the dead.

Whoever will believe in Him can have eternal life.
If you come to Him repenting, He will surely not despise.
When you have lifted up the Son of Man, you'll know that I am He."
Jesus, like the snake, had to be lifted on a tree.
For our sake, God made Him sin, He who knew no sin.
He did become a curse for us, so our souls He could redeem.

Jesus is that Son of man who's lifted on the cross.
Jesus, source of healing, source of rescue to the lost.
Jesus, without sin portrayed as evil and a curse.
An embodiment for sin, with His own life He disbursed.
Everyone, behold His glory as He's lifted on the cross.
Jesus, source of healing, source of rescue to the lost.
"Nicodemus, if you want life, all you have to do is look,
To be rescued from sin's poison as is written in the book.
Blood is flowing, I am hanging, from the cruel cross, just look.
I was dead. I was buried. I rose again. It's in the book."
Nicodemus, Look to Jesus, for salvation, look! Look! Look!
The Son of man is lifted like the snake. It's in the book.

GEORGIA LORAINE CLARKE

> "Ye are the salt of the earth: but if the salt have lost his savour, wherewith shall it be salted? it is thenceforth good for nothing, but to be cast out, and to be trodden under foot of men. Ye are the light of the world. A city that is set on an hill cannot be hid."
> **(Matthew 5:13–14)**

Salt of the Earth

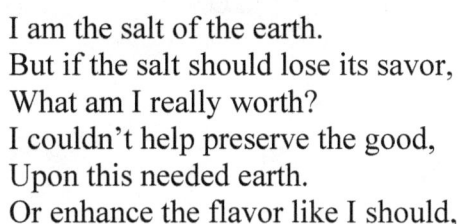

I am the salt of the earth.
But if the salt should lose its savor,
What am I really worth?
I couldn't help preserve the good,
Upon this needed earth.
Or enhance the flavor like I should,
Within my very own neighborhood.
I wouldn't even be in God's favor,
If the salt should lose its savor.
What am I really worth
Upon this needed earth?

I am the light of the world.
But if the light's hid under a bushel,
How can it be unfurled?
The light in me should not be dimmed,
If chosen to light the world.
Then if my light is partly rimmed,
Means of salvation cut and trimmed.
I would be losing something crucial,
If my light's hid under a bushel.
How can it be unfurled
Chosen to light the world?

God chose my vessel for His light.
Therefore, that light was not created
By me or anyone otherwise.
This light through me must be reflected,

And only comes from Christ.
From God to me illuminated,
In me, through me, to be ignited.
Should never be by any means shaded,
Because this light was not created
By me or anyone otherwise.
All praise belongs to Christ!

GEORGIA LORAINE CLARKE

"Let your light so shine before men, that they may see your good works, and glorify your Father which is in heaven."
(Matthew 5:16)

Light to Heaven

Can you imagine if you were a light,
That was shining in a very dark place?
Where people in darkness would follow your light,
Ascertaining sweet saving grace.

Imagine you were a city that's been set upon a hill,
A city that can never be hid,
A city that would stand no matter the gales,
All spoils its beauty forbid.

Can you imagine if your light shined so bright,
Leading sinners to Jesus above?
Your good works – that great light – robustly in sight,
Oh what a signet of love!

Imagine that your light would continue to shine,
Till a world of darkness is lessen.
Your good works drawing sinners to come glorify
The Father, pointing them towards heaven.

"For if I build again the things which I destroyed, I make myself a transgressor. For I through the law am dead to the law, that I might live unto God. I am crucified with Christ: nevertheless I live; yet not I, but Christ liveth in me: and the life which I now live in the flesh I live by the faith of the Son of God, who loved me, and gave himself for me. I do not frustrate the grace of God: for if righteousness come by the law, then Christ is dead in vain."
(Galatians 2:18–21)

GEORGIA LORAINE CLARKE

Possess Me with Your Spirit

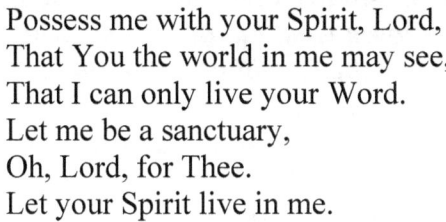

Possess me with your Spirit, Lord,
That You the world in me may see,
That I can only live your Word.
Let me be a sanctuary,
Oh, Lord, for Thee.
Let your Spirit live in me.

>Possess me with your Spirit, Lord,
>So I'd be controlled by Thee,
>So I'll live, and yet not I,
>But the Christ who lives in me.
>Oh Lord, Oh Lord,
>Let your Spirit live in me.

Possess me with your Spirit, Lord,
That through me may shine your light.
Through the power of your Word,
Only to do what's right.
Oh Lord, for Thee
Let Your Spirit live in me.

>Possess me with your Spirit, Lord,
>So I'd be controlled by Thee,
>So I'll live, and yet not I,
>But the Christ who lives in me.
>Oh Lord, Oh Lord,
>Let your Spirit live in me.

"In this was manifested the love of God toward us, because that God sent his only begotten Son into the world, that we might live through him. Herein is love, not that we loved God, but that he loved us, and sent his Son to be the propitiation for our sins. Beloved, if God so loved us, we ought also to love one another. No man hath seen God at any time. If we love one another, God dwelleth in us, and his love is perfected in us."
(1 John 4:9–12)

GEORGIA LORAINE CLARKE

Because God Loves He Gave

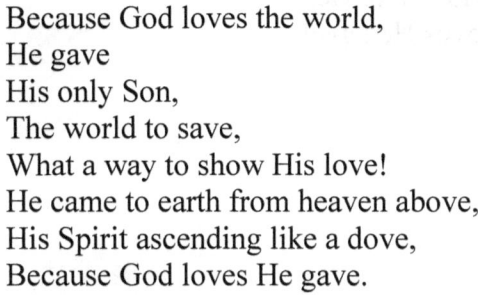

Because God loves the world,
He gave
His only Son,
The world to save,
What a way to show His love!
He came to earth from heaven above,
His Spirit ascending like a dove,
Because God loves He gave.

Today we claim
We follow Christ.
We claim to love,
Yet minimize,
To give unto a suffering soul,
Turn up our noses acting cold,
No sympathy, no heart of gold,
And then proclaim we follow Christ!

We claim we love,
Yet never giving.
Our selfish habits
Are never willing
To actually lend a helping hand,
To a brother who's sinking in the sand.
Our greed put folks on the witness stand.
How can we love yet never giving?

Because God loves the world

MOVING FROM BROKENNESS TO VICTORY

He gave
His only Son
The world to save.
He simply says, "Just follow Me
From this earth to eternity."
To follow is to love like He,
Because God loves He gave!

GEORGIA LORAINE CLARKE

"(As it is written, I have made thee a father of many nations,) before him whom he believed, even God, who quickeneth the dead, and calleth those things which be not as though they were."
(Romans 4:17)

Call Things That Are Not as Though They Were

On the first day of creation, God called light into being
The most incredible thing I had ever seen.
Four days later, God made the sun, moon, and star,
The source for the light, that's a prodigy by far.

So God called the light before He made the source for the light,
With the measure of faith and the Word as insight.
God calls things that are not, as though they were,
A mystical, transcendent, supreme wonder.

Man is limited, man is just natural,
But with this same measure of faith man can be supernatural.
And how do we get that kind of faith? We may ask,
When supernatural ability's such an incredible task.

We can access God's faith through hearing His Word,
But it must be accepted, it can't be demurred.
We have to believe in a God who can't be seen,
And cannot be proven by any natural means.

We must be developed in this supernatural faith,

To truly realize how much we can create.
When we can call things that are not as though they were,
A mystical, transcendent, supreme wonder!

GEORGIA LORAINE CLARKE

"And he said unto me, My grace is sufficient for thee: for my strength is made perfect in weakness. Most gladly therefore will I rather glory in my infirmities, that the power of Christ may rest upon me."
(2 Corinthians 12:9)

GEORGIA LORAINE CLARKE

Rewarder

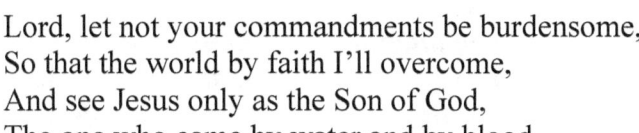

Lord, let not your commandments be burdensome,
So that the world by faith I'll overcome,
And see Jesus only as the Son of God,
The one who came by water and by blood.

For He's a rewarder of those who seek,
His strength made perfect when I am weak.
For He only wants the best for me,
Of peace and expected prosperity.

So I'll seek Him each day with all my heart,
From me he promised He will never depart.
For me He suffered on that cruel cross,
Now all my gains for Him I count but loss.

For He's a rewarder of those who seek,
His strength made perfect when I am weak.
For He only wants the best for me,
Of peace and expected prosperity.

"But the God of all grace, who hath called us unto his eternal glory by Christ Jesus, after that ye have suffered a while, make you perfect, stablish, strengthen, settle you."
(1 Peter 5:10)

GEORGIA LORAINE CLARKE

Beautiful Again

Descendants of the enemies hate,
Mistreated, left in a deserted state.
Day and night blend into one,
Thick blackness eliminates the sun.
But a new day has finally come!
A day that starts the dawning of light,
The glory of God echoes bright.
This city's walls will be rebuilt,
Walls unshakeable, freed from guilt.
Shrubbery assembled by nature's spite,
Its gates will be opened by day and night.
To let in rulers of many nations,
Draining the wealth of foreign kingdoms.
Inviting treasures from across the sea,
Wealth of many nations shall be brought to me.
Victory is the name I will give to the walls,
Sturdy conquest, standing tall.
Praise is the name I will give to the gates,
No more raiders lying in wait.
The sun will no more set nor the moon go down,
A city to be proud of for all time to come.
The mighty God has rescued me,
Scarcity over! Renounced poverty.
Days of sorrows have come to an end,
Violence and ruins will never again,
Be heard of in this city's borders.

MOVING FROM BROKENNESS TO VICTORY

GEORGIA LORAINE CLARKE

Part 6

At Peace

MOVING FROM BROKENNESS TO VICTORY

"And the peace of God, which passeth all understanding, shall keep your hearts and minds through Christ Jesus."
(Philippians 4:7)

GEORGIA LORAINE CLARKE

Happy in this Place

Lord, send Thine hand from above,
Deliver us from great waters deep,
Hover over us like a dove,
Lay us down in peaceful sleep.

Lord, let our garners be full,
Affording all manner of store,
And our oxen be strong to pull,
So we won't be hungry anymore.

Lord, let our sons be as plants,
Grown up as trees tall and strong.
Lord, let our daughters enchant,
With a sense of what's right and wrong.

Lord, a new song we will sing,
And play instruments of many a strings.
Unto thee our praises will ring,
Our Lord, our Savior, our King.

Happy we are in this place,
Our faith, O Lord, you've restored.
Happy to be in such case,
Happy we are in the Lord.

MOVING FROM BROKENNESS TO VICTORY

"In every thing give thanks: for this is the will of God in Christ Jesus concerning you."
(1 Thessalonians 5:18)

Thank God

Thank God for the pain.
Thank God for the rain.
Thank God for the struggles again and again.

Thank God for the haters.
Thank God for the fakers.
Thank God for the many persistent heart breakers.

Thank God for betrayers.
Thank God for degraders.
Thank God for the times I have spent into prayers.

Thank God for the losses.
Thank God for the crosses.
Thank God for deleting all unwanted dross.

Thank God He forgave.
Thank God that He saves.
Thank God that He never allowed me to cave.

Thank God for new hope.
Thank God I could cope.
Thank God that I never did hang myself with the rope.

Thank God for this race.

Thank God I could praise.
Thank God for the access to the sweet throne of grace.

Thank God for the night.
Thank God for the light.
Thank God that His glory shines ever so bright.

Thank God He was there.
Thank God when I feared.
Thank God that sweet victory for sure did appear!

GEORGIA LORAINE CLARKE

MOVING FROM BROKENNESS TO VICTORY

"Acquaint now thyself with him, and be at peace: thereby good shall come unto thee."
(Job 22:21)

GEORGIA LORAINE CLARKE

Assuming My Purpose

Every life has a purpose.
But it took me quite a while
To ascertain my purpose,
And accept it with a smile.

Everyone has unique talents,
And abilities that define
Who he is, all he's made of,
And how he's meant to shine.

I learned that my achievements
Come to me more easily,
When I put love into helping
Even my worst enemies.

In doing so I hail up coals
Of fire on their heads,
And the snares that they have set for me
Have taken them instead.

I incorporate my talents
Into all I have to do,
I have a purpose on this earth,
And I must walk into my shoe.

As I freely assume my purpose
When all is said and done,
I'm fulfilled that I have helped

MOVING FROM BROKENNESS TO VICTORY

To make a difference and then some.

Capitalizing on my purpose
Each day voluntarily
Has made me into whom
God has intended me to be.

GEORGIA LORAINE CLARKE

"Wherefore David blessed the LORD before all the congregation: and David said, Blessed be thou, LORD God of Israel our father, for ever and ever. Thine, O LORD, is the greatness, and the power, and the glory, and the victory, and the majesty: for all that is in the heaven and in the earth is thine; thine is the kingdom, O LORD, and thou art exalted as head above all. Both riches and honour come of thee, and thou reignest over all; and in thine hand is power and might; and in thine hand it is to make great, and to give strength unto all. Now therefore, our God, we thank thee, and praise thy glorious name. But who am I, and what is my people, that we should be able to offer so willingly after this sort? for all things come of thee, and of thine own have we given thee. For we are strangers before thee, and sojourners, as were all our fathers: our days on the earth are as a shadow, and there is none abiding
(1 Chronicles 29:10–15)

GEORGIA LORAINE CLARKE

My Happy Place

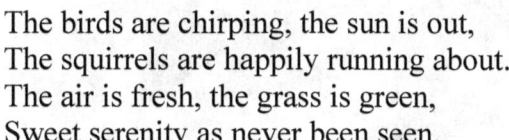

The birds are chirping, the sun is out,
The squirrels are happily running about.
The air is fresh, the grass is green,
Sweet serenity as never been seen.

As the silent wind glides gently along,
The little wren flies by singing a song.
The trees stand tall, the fruits hang low,
Tender the leaves sway to and fro.

The blooming flowers outlay in rows,
Along the grassy meadow flow.
Magnificent colorful petals spread,
Colors of purple, blue, yellow, some red.

Soft fluffy clouds across the sky,
Over shades of blue lightly painted high.
No sign of overcast, no sign of night,
Everything beautiful, everything bright.

The river flows by, it's crystal clear,
No worries, no doubt, no pain, no fear.
God's presence sweeping through the air,
And laughing children everywhere.

MOVING FROM BROKENNESS TO VICTORY

References

From Brokenness to Breakthrough
Retrieved from: www.colleenath.com

www.printerest.com

Nearing Midnight publication
Retrieved from: themidnight-cry.blogspot.com

Walking the Walk / Bartimaeus Quiet…
quietplace4prayer.wordpress.com

Light from the Old Testament – Lesson…
Retrieved from: ubdavid.org

Road to Emmaus
Retrieved from: roadtoemmauspbc.blogspot.com

Scripture Archives – Red Letter Christians
Retrieved from: www.redletterchristians.org

The Evangelista
Retrieved from: theevangelista.com

Life / Rule Your Life
Retrieved from: rituvaghela.wordpress.com

The Dark Hedges

Retrieved from: mononeil.photoshelter.com

Faith / RestinJesus.me
Retrieved from: www.restinjesus.me

Lamb and Lion Ministry
Retrieved from: christinprophecy.org

The Great Famine of Ireland
Retrieved from: www.yourirish.com

Remember This: Jesus is Coming Back on a White Horse
Retrieved from: believeacts2blog.wordpress.com

Lilies Sparrows and Grass
Retrieved from: liliessparrowsandgrass.com

Fighting the Demons of Worship Leader Depression
Retrieved from: www.zachicks.com

Rate of Depression: The Thinking Man's Idiot
Retrieved from: thethinkingmansidiot.wordpress.com

Waters of Noah: When All Else Fails He will never fail you
Retrieved from: watersofnoah.blogspot.com

Through the Window of Pinterest
Retrieved from: www.pinterest.com

The Disciple MD – Inspirational Daily Quote

Retrieved from: thedisciplemd.com

Principles for Life – November 2013
Retrieved from: principlesforlifeministries.com

Protected by the Wall of Fire: Prayers and Promises
Retrieved from: dianarasmussen.com

Jen's World: L'amour de Dieu est folie
Retrieved from:
thissimplyamazingworld.blogspot.com

The Introvert's Brain: Why they might "think too much"
Retrieved from: tinybuddha.com

15 Myths about Introverts: In 3 Words
Retrieved from: lonerwolf.com

Metal Door is so metal
Retrieved from: metaldoorissometal.tumblr.com

Worship / Light to live by
Retrieved from: Jkitchen.org

August 27th Thought of the Day /
Retrieved from: realchitchat.org

Audio Bible Study
Retrieved from: www.ordination.org

Limiting You Capacity to Receive Limits your Life
Retrieved from:www.radiantsurvivor.com

Pray for the Peace of Jerusalem: 3/5/13 Prayer
Retrieved from: www.freerepublic.com

How Many Times Do U Thank God? /
Retrieved from: dephnevictorious.wordpress.com

Overcoming Loneliness – Finding Purpose in the Midst of Pain
Retrieved from: https://overcomingloneliness.com/

Faith: Overcoming the Addiction to Smoking
Retrieved from: https://quitday.org/support/faith-religion/

Wings as Eagle: Being One with the Lord
Retrieved from: starchecenter.net

Eagle's Wings by Jack E. Dawson
Retrieved from: www.jackdawson.com

www.shalomevangelicalministries.org

The Source of Our Strength
Retrieved from: http://www.sfltimes.com/opinion/the-source-of-our-strength

The Real Exodus Story
Retrieved from: realtruth.org

Jesus Walks on the Water: Prepare for Mass

Retrieved from:
https://prepareformass.wordpress.com/category/jesus-walks-on-the-water/

Blog Post – AOE Ministries
Retrieved from:
http://www.aoeministries.org/whats-going-on---events-encouragement-education--more/previous/2

Christ in the Home of Mary and Martha
https://www.lds.org/media-library/images/jesus-mary-martha-396319?lang=eng

Thursday of Length: John 11: 17-27
Retrieved from:
http://giveusthisdaydevotional.com/give-us-this-day/thursday-of-lent-2-john-1117-27/

Lift Up Your Eyes: Well of Salvation
Retrieved from:
http://www.wellofsalvation.com/lift-up-your-eyes/

Grace is the Place of Rest - Anatoliy Orgunov
Retrieved from:https://www.linkedin.com/pulse/20141024135355-95807042-grace-is-the-place-of-rest

Signs and Wonders – Jesus
Retrieved from: http://justadisciple.org/signs--wonders.html

Jonathan Edwards – Regeneration, Repentance and Reformation

Retrieved from:
https://regenerationandrepentance.wordpress.com/tag/jonathan-edwards/

Hello Wisdom
Posted by Gayle Nobel on October 8, 2015
Retrieved from: http://www.gaylenobel.com/hello-wisdom/

Quotes of Wisdom – Built to Inspire
Retrieved from:
http://www.builttoinspire.com/wisdom-quotes/

North America: Life's Big and Small Adventures
Retrieved from:
http://lifesbigandsmalladventures.com/category/north-america/

Living in the Present Moment – Spiritual Living Institute
Retrieved from:
http://spirituallivinginstitute.org/live-present-moment/

Good Things: March 2013
Retrieved from:
http://jorpins.blogspot.com/2013_03_01_archive.html

Picking Up the Bible – D. L. Moody – For the Love of His Truth

Retrieved from: http://fortheloveofhistruth.com/2011/03/16/picking-up-the-bible/

Is It Irresponsible To Trust God Too Much? (2011)
Retrieved from: http://jenniferfulwiler.com/2011/03/is-it-irresponsible-to-trust-god-too-much/

Ego and Humility
Retrieved from: http://www.brightertomorrow.net/humility.htm

Dana's Short Devotions: Enduring the Trials of Temptations
Retrieved from:http://www.christian-resources-today.com/short-devotions-13.html

Experiencing God / Educator
Retrieved from: educator.wordpress.com

DaeLight Foundations
Retrieved from: www.daelf.com

Michael Hyatt. (2011). Your Most Important Leadership Tool – 3 Reasons Why you Must Guard Your Heart
Retrieved From: http://michaelhyatt.com/three-reasons-why-you-must-guard-your-heart.html

Amira – Avalon Teaching

Retrieved from: http://avalonteachings.com/about-avalon/
Consider it all Joy (2010).
Retrieved from: http://www.consideringitalljoy.com/2010_05_01_archive.html

Clyde Rathbone
Retrieved from: https://www.quora.com/What-are-the-most-common-life-mistakes-young-people-make

Carol Kingsley (2016). Writing with a Purpose
Retrieved from: http://carolkinsey.net/

Christianity – Faith in God, Jesus Christ
Retrieved from: http://www.christianity.com/

From Depth to the Wilderness – Whom shall walk with us? (2014).
Retrieved from: http://depthstowilderness.com/whom-shall-walk-with-us/

Poetry Hope/ African Plato
Retrieved from: http://www.africanplato.com/poetry-hope/

Umead – A Ray of Hope
Retrieved from: http://kodeforest.com/html/umeed/

Holy Spirit – Disciples of Faith

https://disciplesofhope.wordpress.com/category/holy-spirit/

Overcoming Depression One Day at a Time
Retrieved from:
http://www.kamajensen.com/overcoming-depression-one-day-at-time/

Fancy Free Flaneur
https://www.pinterest.com/theweekendguide/fancy-free-flaneur/

The Mighty Army of the 144,000: The Great Harvest is Coming, Part 2.
Retrieved from:
http://mightywarriorsofyah.com/2015/09/21/the-mighty-army-of-the-144000-the-great-harvest-is-coming/

Putting On Christ – OLGCBlog
Retrieved from: http://www.olgcblog.com/putting-on-christ-jesus/

Maranatha Trumpeter – Rapture Message – The Blessed Hope
Retrieved from:
https://rapturewatcher.wordpress.com/tag/rapture-message/

Pastor Bill Stevenson. (2014). Mesquite Citizen Journal - *The Prayer Jesus Prayed*

Retrieved from:
http://mesquitecitizen.com/viewnews.php?newsid=7420&id=60

Highlight of the World Cup – God magazine
Retrieved from:
http://www.godisreal.today/highlight.html
Bible Guide for the New Age – 2 Cor. 4:16 (2013).
The Inward Man is Eternal
Retrieved from:
http://bibleguidefornewage.blogspot.com/2014/07/2-corinthians-416-inward-man-is-eternal.html

Cathy Severson (2014). Mindfulness – The Ability to Live in the Here and Now
Retrieved from:
http://www.retirewow.com/mindfulness-the-ability-to-live-in-the-here-and-now/

Whispers for the Soul – Touching Your Heart and Soul (2012)
Retrieved from:
https://whispersforthesoul.com/page/54/

Ronnie Christian.com – Making Disciples Who Make Disciples
Retrieved from:
http://www.ronniechristian.com/2010_01_01_archive.html

Ancient Christian Wisdom (2015)
ancientchristianwisdom.com

The Love of a Brother Poor Homeless Boys
Retrieved from:
https://www.pinterest.com/pin/397161260865591331/

Pray for the Hostages (2011)
Retrieved from:
http://prayforthehostages.blogspot.com/

Repilique
http://repliqueministry.org/

Rejoice Quotes like Success
Retrieved from: Likesuccess.com

Jesus Will Open the Gate to Heaven

https://www.pinterest.com/pin/94434923406429961/

Yaira Robinson. The Problem with Noah (2013)
Retrieved from:
http://www.stateofformation.org/2013/10/the-problem-with-noah/

Austin Cline. Noah's Art, The Flood and the Curse of Canaan, Ham's Son
Retrieved from:
http://atheism.about.com/od/bibleinpicturesimages/ig/Noah-Ark-Flood/

Bv53846.png

http://www.consciousnessis.net/Children_Of_Serpent.html

Lectio da Sexta-feira da paixão do Senhor: Jo 18, 1-19, 1-42
Retrieved from:
http://blog.comshalom.org/rapaduraespiritual/lectio-da-sexta-feira-da-paixao-senhor-jo-18-1-19-1-42/

Living in the Shadow of His Hand (2014)
Retrieved from:
http://www.livingintheshadowofhishand.com/2014/07/look-and-live.html
Ronnie Christian. Com – Good for Nothing Salt
Retrieved from:
http://www.ronniechristian.com/2009_06_01_archive.html

Nature Archives – Wow Amazing
Retrieved from:
http://www.wowamazing.com/lifestyle/nature/

Turn Your Eyes upon Jesus
Retrieved from:
https://www.pinterest.com/pin/186336503306621710/

A Hopeful Life (2009)
Retrieved from:
http://jesuscristoesmivida.blogspot.com/2009_05_01_archive.html

Might Scripture

Retrieved from:
http://www.mightyscripture.com/galations-2.html

Benjamin K. Phillips Blog – A Ray of Hope
Retrieved from:
https://benjaminkphilip.wordpress.com/
Heart of a Missionary Being the Feet of Jesus
Retrieved from:
http://breannarains.blogspot.com/2012/02/happy-valentines-day.html

Thieves & Priests – Attitudes in the Good Samaritan Parable (2013).
Retrieved from: http://gregburdine.com/tag/selfish

Justin Steckbauer (2014). Big Picture: The Solution to all the Problems of Earth
Retrieved from:
https://libertychurchonline.wordpress.com/2014/11/04/big-picture-the-solution-to-all-the-problems-of-earth/

Gospel for America – The Will of God
Retrieved from:
http://www.gospelsforamerica.com/gospels-for-america-the-will-of-god.html

Genesis – God is Creator: Genesis1
Retrieved from:
https://www.pinterest.com/pin/512988213775630179/

A Safe Harbor in Jesus: A Warm Welcome to a Safe Harbor
Retrieved from:
https://1safeharborisjesus.wordpress.com/page/4/

Well this is What I Think (2016).
Retrieved from: https://wellthisiswhatithink.com/

Jerusalem
http://www.liberallifestyles.com/?p=63099

Bible Study #61: The Concept of "Peace"
https://ivarfjeld.com/2015/08/20/bible-study-61-the-multiple-understanding-of-the-concept-of-peace/

Finding the Peace of God in the Midst of the Storm
Retrieved from:
https://heartofworshipchurch.wordpress.com/2015/05/04/finding-the-peace-of-god-in-the-midst-of-the-storm/

Praying in the Powerful Name of Jesus
Retrieved from:
http://www.crosswalk.com/faith/prayer/praying-in-the-powerful-name-of-jesus.html

5 Things You Should Know About How God Sees You – A Bible Study by Jack Kelley
Retrieved from: https://gracethrufaith.com/topical-studies/spiritual-life/5-things-you-should-know-about-how-god-sees-you/

Brown Pelican Society of Louisiana

Retrieved from: http://brownpelicanla.com/

My New Beginnings
Retrieved from:
https://www.pinterest.com/bethg2208/my-new-beginning-/

Pastor Tommy (2013) Personal Peace Plan
Retrieved from:
https://tommyboland.com/2013/03/14/personal-peace-plan/

Paradise on Pinterest
Retrieved from:
https://www.pinterest.com/bwynita/paradise/

Jeremy Myers. Fishing with Jesus

Retrieved from:

https://redeeminggod.com/sermons/luke/luke_5_1-

To Contact

Georgia Loraine Clarke

for speaking engagements

Please send all inquiries to
georgialoraine@yahoo.com,

717-608-8681

Visit her website at

www.georgialorainebooks.com

GEORGIA LORAINE CLARKE

www.ingramcontent.com/pod-product-compliance
Lightning Source LLC
Chambersburg PA
CBHW070645160426
43194CB00009B/1591